Mamenchisaurus

Written by Rupert Oliver
Illustrated by Andrew Howatt

Library of Congress Cataloging in Publication Data

Oliver, Rupert.
  Mamenchisaurus.

  Summary: Follows a long-necked plant eater through
his day as he becomes separated from his herd,
encounters other dinosaurs, and finally rejoins his
own kind.
  1. Mamenchisaurus—Juvenile literature.
[1. Mamenchisaurus. 2. Dinosaurs] I. Howatt, Andrew,
ill. II. Title.
QE862.S3O455   1986   567.9'7   85-28336
ISBN 0-86592-220-9

Rourke Enterprises, Inc.
Vero Beach, FL 32964

Dimorphodon

Brachiosaurus

Dilophosaurus

Lystrosaurus

Rutiodon

Mamenchisaurus

Mamenchisaurus

Plateosaurus

Chasmosaurus

Protoceratops

It had been raining even before the sun had risen. It was almost noon and the rain was still falling. Mamenchisaurus bit off a tasty mouthful of leaves from the high branches of the tree. He chewed them quickly and then swallowed them, taking another mouthful as he did so. Mamenchisaurus was always hungry and spent most of his time eating.

Around the small clump of trees at which
Mamenchisaurus was feeding stood the rest of his
herd. Mamenchisaurus looked around to make sure
they were still there. He always felt safer when he
was near his herd. The rain was not falling quite so
heavily now and a ray of sunshine burst through the
clouds.

Mamenchisaurus caught sight of some tasty leaves near the top of a tree further into the woods. He moved forward to get near enough to eat them. As Mamenchisaurus pushed through the dense undergrowth, he realized that he was on the edge of a river bank. Mamenchisaurus moved forward and then he felt the ground fall slightly. He looked around in alarm as the river bank gave way beneath his great weight.

He slithered down a steep, muddy
slope until he reached the bottom.

Mamenchisaurus roared out a distress signal
and the herd appeared at the top of the slope.
Mamenchisaurus tried to climb up the slope, but the
mud was too slippery.

The other Mamenchisaurs found they could
not help him, so, after a while, they moved back
to the trees to continue eating. Mamenchisaurus felt
very alone. He had never been away from the herd
before and he felt vulnerable. He had to get back to
his herd. He tried climbing the slope again, but just
slithered back down. Perhaps there would be a way
out further along the river.

Mamenchisaurus splashed along the river, his
feet sinking into the ooze with each step. Suddenly a
small Gongubusaurus dashed from among a small
clump of horsetails and scampered up the river bank.
Mamenchisaurus could also climb the bank here, for
the slope did not seem to be as steep.

Treading very carefully, Mamenchisaurus managed to heave his great bulk up the steep slope without sliding backward. Mamenchisaurus looked around for his herd, but it was nowhere in sight. Mamenchisaurus began to plod off in the direction from which he had come. Perhaps he would find his herd that way.

Mamenchisaurus had not gone very far when two huge shapes emerged from some trees in front of him. At once he recognized the large creatures as Yangchuanosaurs. Mamenchisaurus was very frightened because Yangchuanosaurs were ferocious hunters which were always ready to make a meal of plant eaters such as Mamenchisaurus.

Mamenchisaurus turned to move away, but the Yangchuanosaurs had already seen him. The hunters were hungry and could run faster than Mamenchisaurus could walk. Soon they began to overtake him. Mamenchisaurus knew that he could not escape. He only had one chance.

He stood still with his back toward the advancing hunters and waited. The fierce looking Yangchuanosaurs came running forward, with their fearsome jaws and claws, eager for an easy meal.

When they were almost upon Mamenchisaurus, he lashed out with his tail. The swinging tail caught one of the Yangchuanosaurs just below its arm and lifted it right off its feet. The force of the blow knocked the dinosaur sideways and sent it sprawling heavily on the ground. The second hunter stopped in amazement and quickly backed out of range of Mamenchisaurus' tail.

The Yangchuanosaurus which the frightened Mamenchisaurus had hit lay on the ground moaning in pain. The other hunter came forward to help its companion but did not attempt any attack on Mamenchisaurus. Mamenchisaurus moved off, but kept a careful eye on the Yangchuanosaurs because they might still try to attack again.

Mamenchisaurus was worried. He wanted to rejoin his herd, but the Yangchuanosaurs were between him and the herd. Then, he saw a group of sauropods in the distance. Perhaps his herd had moved. Mamenchisaurus moved toward the sauropods, passing a Tuojiangosaurus on his way.

As Mamenchisaurus approached the group of sauropods he realized that something was wrong. They were staring at Mamenchisaurus and growling angrily. One of the largest dinosaurs from the herd came lumbering forward and shook its head at Mamenchisaurus, bellowing. Mamenchisaurus stopped in puzzlement and looked more closely at the sauropods. He realized that this was not his herd. The sauropods were Zigongosaurs. They had some young with them and did not want to be disturbed.

Mamenchisaurus did not want any trouble so he moved away from the Zigongosaurs, taking care not to stray toward the Yangchuanosaurus.

Mamenchisaurus lumbered on across the countryside until he came to the top of a low rise. From the hill he could see out across the landscape and he looked for his herd. Mamenchisaurus was suddenly startled when something leaped from the undergrowth. It was only a Sinocoelurus chasing a small mammal. Fortunately, it was no danger to Mamenchisaurus. As Mamenchisaurus gazed out from his hill he saw a group of sauropods emerge from some trees. The sauropods looked like other Mamenchisaurs. Perhaps this was his herd.

Mamenchisaurus moved down the slope in the direction of the herd.

Mamenchisaurus plodded slowly across the ground and roared out a signal of recognition. This was his herd. The members of the herd turned around when they heard Mamenchisaurus roar. As they realized that this was their missing member they, too, roared in recognition.

It was getting near to evening now, and the rain clouds were beginning to build up again. The herd looked for somewhere to rest for the night. There was a small clump of trees nearby and they moved toward it. Mamenchisaurus had not eaten for some time and was very hungry indeed. While the rest of the herd settled down to sleep, Mamenchisaurus continued to eat in order to satisfy his hunger. It was dark and the moon was high in the sky before Mamenchisaurus settled down to sleep.

Mamenchisaurus and Late Jurassic China

Skeleton of Mamenchisaurus

Length: 72 feet
Length of neck: 36 feet

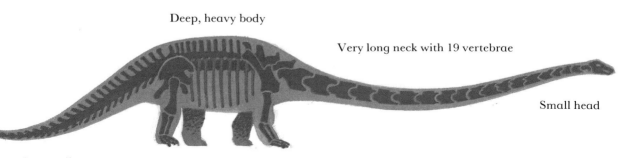

Deep, heavy body

Very long neck with 19 vertebrae

Small head

Long tail

Strong, pillar-like legs to support great weight

Family tree of Mamenchisaurus

Mamenchisaurus belonged to one of the largest and oldest groups of dinosaurs, the sauropods. Sauropods first appeared at the very start of the Jurassic period and survived right through to the end of the Age of Dinosaurs. All sauropods shared similar characteristics: they were all large, all had long necks, all had long tails and they were all plant eaters. At about 72 feet long, Mamenchisaurus was one of the largest sauropods. It certainly had the longest neck of any known dinosaur, with 19 neck vertebrae. The sauropods belonged to the saurischia, or lizard-hipped, group of dinosaurs. All the meat eating dinosaurs and a small group of dinosaurs called the prosauropods belonged to this category. All other dinosaurs had a bird-like hip and so are known as ornithischia. After the time of Mamenchisaurus, the ornithischia became increasingly important as plant eaters and sauropods became rarer and smaller.

The world of Mamenchisaurus

In the time of Mamenchisaurus, China, like the world as a whole, was very different from how it is today. All the continents were in different positions on the globe and many oceans did not exist. This meant that most of the land was joined together into one large continent across which animals could roam freely. The plant life of the period was also very different. There were no flowers and no grass, nor were there many other plants which we would recognize today. Among the strange plants of that time were cycads, giant ferns, Williamsonias and many different species of horsetails. There were the familiar conifer trees and small ferns which continue to exist to this day.

In the animal world in those days, birds and mammals were unimportant compared with their position today. Mammals had evolved many millions of years earlier, but they were still small, insignificant animals. Birds had only recently appeared and were probably clumsy fliers which could not compete with the reptilian pterosaurs which filled the skies. The land really belonged to the dinosaurs. Most of the animals encountered by Mamenchisaurus in the story were dinosaurs which lived in China at that time. Gongubusaurus was a small bird-hipped dinosaur which ate low growing vegetation and could run quickly. Yangchuanosaurus was a large, powerful dinosaur whose large claws and sharp teeth tell scientists that this was a ferocious hunter, probably quite capable of killing and eating a Mamenchisaurus. It was about 33 feet long and was related to the more famous Allosaurus. As can be guessed from its appearance, Tuojiangosaurus belonged to the same family as the well known Stegosaurus which was living in North America at that time. Tuojiangosaurus was another bird-hipped dinosaur, like Gongubusaurus. Mamenchisaurus was not the only sauropod to live in China at this time. It had to compete for food with Zigongosaurus which was named after the place where its fossils have been found. One of the smallest dinosaurs of the time was Sinocoelurus, whose name means "Chinese hollow-tail". Scientists have found only four teeth from this animal. No bones have ever been found. Since the teeth are very similar to those of a dinosaur then living in America, scientists can be reasonably sure of what Sinocoelurus looked like and how it lived.

When did Mamenchisaurus live?

Mamenchisaurus lived during the Age of the Dinosaurs. Scientists call this stretch of time the Mesozoic Era, which means "Middle Life". This era has been divided into three periods. First, the Triassic, which began about 225 million years ago and lasted for 35 million years. Second, the Jurassic, which began 190 million years ago and ended about 136 million years ago. The Final period is called the Cretaceous, and it ended some 65 million years ago. Mamenchisaurus fossils have been found in the most recent Jurassic rocks. This means that it lived about 140 million years ago.

Home of Mamenchisaurus

The fossils of Mamenchisaurus were found by scientists near to the town of Mamenchi in China. The dinosaur gained its name, which means "lizard from Mamenchi", because it was found near that town. Mamenchisaurus belonged to a group of dinosaurs known as diplodocids. It is unusual to have a diplodocid from Asia. Most diplodocids came from America, Europe or Africa.

The life of Mamenchisaurus

Mamenchisaurus became extinct many millions of years before the first man walked on earth. This means that there are no records of any human having ever seen a Mamenchisaurus. However, scientists can discover much about a dinosaur from its bones and teeth and can guess at how it lived. Mamenchisaurus had no natural weapons with which to attack other animals and its teeth were simple and peg-like. This means that it ate plants. Its enormous size and long neck indicate which sort of plants it ate. Mamenchisaurus probably used its long neck to reach high into the trees for food other dinosaurs were too short to eat. The strong legs and relatively small feet indicate that Mamenchisaurus walked on hard, dry ground. It did not spend much time in swamps. Danger sometimes theatened in the shape of fierce, meat eating dinosaurs. At times like that, Mamenchisaurus would bunch together and lash out their tails. Because of its large size and small mouth Mamenchisaurus probably had to spend most of its time eating in order to survive.

Two other sauropods from the Jurassic period.

Brachiosaurus

Apatosaurus

The Fearless Flights
of Hazel Ying Lee

For Madeleine, Justin, and Elizabeth —J.L.

To my *umma.* Your love, strength,
and courage inspire me every day. —J.K.

Little, Brown and Company
Hachette Book Group
1290 Avenue of the Americas, New York, NY 10104
Visit us at LBYR.com

First Edition: February 2021

Little, Brown and Company is a division of Hachette Book Group, Inc.
The Little, Brown name and logo are trademarks of Hachette Book Group, Inc.

The publisher is not responsible for websites (or their content) that are not owned by the publisher.

Library of Congress Control Number: 2019945911

ISBN 978-0-7595-5495-5

PRINTED IN MALAYSIA

TWP

10 9 8 7 6 5 4 3 2 1

THE FEARLESS FLIGHTS OF HAZEL YING LEE

By Julie Leung

Illustrated by Julie Kwon

Little, Brown and Company

New York   Boston

Hazel Ying Lee was born fearless.
She was not afraid of wind or water,
as the old Cantonese saying goes.

Little Hazel was always the first to jump into the swimming pool.
She would hit the ball the hardest in handball games.

Hazel didn't care that she was not allowed in certain parts of town
or that she had to carry identification on her at all times.

She would run footraces against her brothers,
pushing her legs to go their fastest.

And when Hazel ran out of breath,
she would fall back onto a soft patch of grass
and turn her face toward the sky.

Sometimes on sunny days,
a silver plane would streak across the clouds.
She wondered what it might be like to move so fast
her feet couldn't touch the ground.

It came as no surprise then, that the moment she took her first airplane ride, Hazel Ying Lee knew where she belonged.

She delighted in the way the plane rumbled down the runway, building speed as the engine roared in her ears.

The wheels lifted, and the wind buoyed the metal wings up.
Hazel looked out the window in wonder.

When the plane landed back on the runway like a skipping rock,
Hazel stepped out with only the horizon in her eyes.

"I will be a pilot!" Hazel declared to anyone
who would listen.

"But it's just not ladylike!" her mama warned.

It was 1932, and less than one percent of pilots were women.
But Hazel cared about that least of all.
She wanted to do something
that no other Chinese American girl had done.

Her mother threw her hands up in the air.
"Ai-ya, you're not afraid of anything!"

Once Hazel had a taste of sky,
she couldn't let it go.

To pay for flying lessons, Hazel
worked as an elevator operator
at a department store.

It was one of the few jobs
Chinese girls were allowed to have.

"Invisible jobs," Hazel called them.
Jobs where you were ignored.

Every day in an airless box,
she shuttled shoppers
from one floor to the next.

When she pulled the lever
for different floors, she smiled,
imagining she was moving
a plane's throttle instead.

After work, Hazel chased every chance
to get into the pilot's seat, where she learned to

loop the loops,
roll like a barrel,
and spin in spirals!

In under a year, she earned her flying license.
But what could she do with it?
Americans didn't want to hire the Chinese.
And who would hire a Chinese girl pilot?

Then in 1941, World War II reached American shores with the bombing of Pearl Harbor.

All available male pilots were called to fight overseas.

The US military developed a new program
to train women to fly on the home front:
the Women Airforce Service Pilots—also known as the WASPs!

Hazel knew this was her chance
to become a pilot at last.

She signed up right away,
becoming the first Chinese
American woman to fly
for the US military.

Though they were not allowed to fight on the front lines, WASP work could be just as dangerous. Hazel and her fellow WASPs tested planes straight off the assembly line.

They were the first to fly them,
before any man did, and often
the first to discover
manufacturing defects.

One day, in the middle of a mission, Hazel's engine cut out
mid-flight. The plane shuddered and began to fall.
She relied on her training, crash-landing in a Kansas field.
A farmer nearby mistook her for a Japanese fighter
and chased her, ready to fight.

Hazel ducked under the wing for safety, and shouted that
she was an American. She was finally able to convince the farmer.
"Well, you sure made a pretty landing," he said, begrudgingly.

Hazel told this story to her fellow pilots to make them laugh.
But her own laughter masked a secret heartache. She wondered,
even despite her fearlessness, if she would ever be seen as an
American in other people's eyes.

When she was in the air, however, none of it mattered.
Hazel Ying Lee was one of few women, even among the
WASPs, qualified to fly pursuit planes—
high-powered single-engine fighter jets.
As Hazel zoomed across the sky at hundreds of
miles per hour, America became a patchwork of colors.
Blue mountains melted into green hills and golden plains.
Silver rivers split into gray creeks.

No one could see her eyes, hair, or skin color
when Hazel was thousands of feet above.
Up here, people were just tiny specks against a vast land.
And inside her cockpit, Hazel felt like a dragon
chasing down the sun.
She leaned into the wind, pushing her plane to go faster.
She looked at the horizon, and willed the world
to move forward.

She died of her injuries two days later.
Her family and fellow pilots mourned her passing.
They wanted to honor a life that was brief,
but bold, brave, and bright.

Because WASPs were considered civilians at the time, Hazel was not given military recognition.

The cemetery tried to stop Hazel's family from burying her in the spot they wanted.

They did not want to bury
Chinese in a whites-only cemetery.

Not even heroes.

But Hazel's family believed in *feng shui*,
the Chinese philosophy that one must be in
harmony with one's surroundings.

Translated, *feng* means wind, *shui* means water.
Hazel had never been afraid of either,
as the Cantonese saying goes.

And Hazel deserved so much better than
barriers and boundaries.

The family fought the cemetery's rules, and wrote
a letter to President Franklin Roosevelt in protest.

They willed the world to move forward for Hazel,

and won.

Today, Hazel Ying Lee is remembered in a place chosen just for her
on a hillside overlooking gentle river waters
where the wind blows gently down a slope,
and beckons you to chase the sky.

AUTHOR'S NOTE

Hazel Ying Lee was born August 24, 1912, in Portland, Oregon, during an era of rampant discrimination and racial bias against Chinese people living in the United States. One of eight siblings, it was clear from an early age that Hazel would not let the prejudices of her time stop her from what she wanted to achieve. Hazel loved to run races against her brothers, play handball, and swim.

At age nineteen, Hazel took her first flight with a friend during an air show. From that moment on, Hazel fell in love with flying. She immediately joined the Chinese Flying Club of Portland, one of only two women to do so. She worked as an elevator operator in a department store to help pay for flying lessons. She logged as many hours in the sky as she could, earning her pilot's license within a year.

In 1941, World War II reached US shores with the bombing of Pearl Harbor. All able-bodied male pilots were drafted to the front lines. However, the Air Force still needed more pilots. In 1943, the government established the Women Airforce Service Pilots (WASPs) to train female pilots in order to free up male pilots for combat.

Hazel saw her chance to make a difference in the war effort, doing what she loved to do most—fly.

Out of the 25,000 women who applied and 1,879 who were accepted into the program, Hazel was one of 1,074 who completed the training to become a full-fledged WASP.

As much as it was exciting and liberating, the life of a WASP was also grueling and dangerous. These women tested aircraft right off the assembly lines and ferried the planes all over the country to be shipped overseas. The pilots often worked seven days a week. And though they made important contributions to the war effort, they were not offered military status nor military benefits. Despite these conditions, fellow WASPs fondly remember Hazel as the life of the party—one who loved practical jokes and seeking out the best Chinese restaurants wherever they had layovers.

Hazel was also one of 132 women capable of "flying pursuit," meaning she was qualified to pilot superfast and powerful fighter planes such as P-63 Kingcobras. On Thanksgiving day in 1944, Hazel and her fellow pilots were scheduled to land a number of these planes in Great Falls, Montana. A miscommunication from the radio tower caused Hazel and another pilot to try to land at the same time. The planes collided, and Hazel died from her injuries two days later, at the age of 32.

Three days later, news arrived from France that her brother, Victor, had also died in combat. Her family had to fight to bury Hazel and Victor in the plot of their choice, after being told they were not permitted to be buried in a whites-only cemetery. The family eventually prevailed by writing a letter of protest to President Franklin D. Roosevelt. Hazel was the last WASP to die in service to her country during World War II.

In 1977, President Jimmy Carter finally gave the WASPs veteran status. And in 2009, President Barack Obama awarded all WASPs the Congressional Gold Medal in recognition of their service. "The Women Airforce Service Pilots courageously answered their country's call in a time of need while blazing a trail for the brave women who have given and continue to give so much in service to this nation since," he said during the ceremony.

I first found out about Hazel Ying Lee while visiting the Museum of Chinese in America in New York City. As part of the main exhibit, there stands a wall covered with portraits of notable Chinese Americans. I often like to browse through their faces and wonder at all the little-known histories that were not taught to me as a kid.

Hazel's portrait in particular stood out to me. There was something fearless and determined in her eyes, an expression I couldn't forget. As I learned more about her story, I marveled at Hazel's bravery and passion to pursue the skies, regardless of the gender and racial barriers she faced. I saw a woman who deserved a place in the storybooks.

"She didn't care if it was ladylike or not," her sister Frances Tong has said in interviews about Hazel's love of flying. "She enjoyed the danger and doing something that was new to Chinese girls."

LEARN MORE ABOUT HAZEL YING LEE AND HER FELLOW WASPS

Books

Deng, Sally. *Skyward: The Story of Female Pilots in WWII*. London: Flying Eye Books, 2018.

O'Brien, Keith. *Fly Girls: How Five Daring Women Defied All Odds and Made Aviation History*. New York: Eamon Dolan/Houghton Mifflin Harcourt, 2018.

Williams, Vera S. *WASPs: Women Airforce Service Pilots of World War II*. Osceola, WI: Motorbooks International, 1994.

Documentaries

Rosenberg, Alan H., director. *A Brief Flight: Hazel Ying Lee and the Women Who Flew Pursuit*. A LAWAS Films Production, 2003.

Websites

NBC News. "Remembering Hazel Lee, the first Chinese-American female military pilot": https://www.nbcnews.com/news/asian-america/ remembering-hazel-lee-first-chinese-american- female-military-pilot-n745851

Los Angeles Times. "Chinese American WASP Losing Her Anonymity": https://www.latimes.com/archives/ la-xpm-2003-may-11-adna-pilot11-story.html

1859 Oregon's Magazine. "Sky's The Limit": https://1859oregonmagazine.com/think-oregon/art- culture/hazel-lee/

Museums

Museum of Chinese in America, Hazel Ying Lee Collection: https://www.mocanyc.org

National WASP WWII Museum: https:// waspmuseum.org

Texas Woman's University's Women's Air Force Pilots Collection: https://twu.edu/library/womans- collection/collections/women-airforce-service-pilots/